STRUM & SING

Billie Eilish

Cover photo by Steven Ferdman/Getty Images

ISBN 978-1-7051-31459

HAL•LEONARD®

Visit Hal Leonard Online at
www.halleonard.com

Contact us:
Hal Leonard
7777 West Bluemound Road
Milwaukee, WI 53213
Email: info@halleonard.com

In Europe, contact:
Hal Leonard Europe Limited
42 Wigmore Street
Marylebone, London, W1U 2RN
Email: info@halleonardeurope.com

In Australia, contact:
Hal Leonard Australia Pty. Ltd.
4 Lentara Court
Cheltenham, Victoria, 3192 Australia
Email: info@halleonard.com.au

Bad Guy

Words and Music by
Billie Eilish O'Connell and Finneas O'Connell

(Capo 3rd fret)

Em   Am   B7

Intro

Em | | | |
Am | |B7 | ||

Verse 1

Em | |
White shirt now red: my bloody nose.

| |
Sleeping. You're on your tippy toes,
Am | |
Creeping around like no one knows.
B7 | ||
Think you're so crim - inal.

Verse 2

Em | |
Bruises on both my knees for you.

|
Don't say thank you or please.
|Am | |
I do what I want, when I'm wanting to.
B7 |N.C.
My soul, so cyn - ical.

Chorus 1

‖ **Em** |
So you're a tough guy, "I like it really rough" guy,

|
"I just can't get enough" guy,

|
"Chest always so puffed" guy.

| **Am** |
I'm that bad type, "make your mama sad" type,

| **B7**
"Make your girlfriend mad" type,

| **N.C.**
"Might seduce your dad" type.

| | ‖
I'm the bad guy. *Duh*.

Interlude 1

Em | | |
| **Am** | | **B7** | ‖
I'm the bad guy.

Verse 3

N.C.(Em) | |
I like it when you take control.

| | **(Am)**
Even if you know that you don't own me,

| |
I'll let you play the role:
(B7) | ‖
I'll be your an - imal.

Verse 4

Em | |
My mommy likes to sing along with me,

| |
But she won't sing this song.
Am |
If she reads all the lyrics,

| **B7** | **N.C.**
She'll pity the men I know.

Chorus 2

Repeat Chorus 1

Interlude 2   **Em** | | |

                  |**Am** | |**B7** |
I'm the bad guy.

               |**Em** | | |
Duh.

                             |**Am** | |
I'm only good at playing bad,

B7 | **N.C.**| ‖
Bad.

Outro   ‖:**N.C.(Em)** | :‖

                                              | |
I like it when you get mad.

                                   | |
I guess I'm pretty glad that you're alone.

                           |
You said she's scared of me?

                   |
I mean, I don't see what she sees,

                          | | |
But maybe it's 'cause I'm wearing your cologne.

                   | |
I'm the bad guy.

          | |
Ha!

                  |
I'm, I'm the bad guy,

          |
Bad guy.

      ‖
Ha!

Everything I Wanted

Words and Music by
Billie Eilish O'Connell and Finneas O'Connell

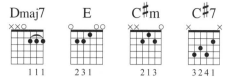

Intro

‖: **Dmaj7**　**E** │　　　│ **C♯m**　**Dmaj7**│　　　　:‖

Verse 1

Dmaj7　**E**　│　　　│ **C♯m**
　　　　I had a dream
　　　　　　Dmaj7│　　　│
I got every - thing I　wanted.
　　　　　E　　│　　│ **C♯m**
Not what you'd think,
　　　　Dmaj7│
And if I'm being　　honest,
　　　　　　　│　　　　**E**　│
It might have been a nightmare
　　　　　│ **C♯m**　　　**Dmaj7**│　　　　‖
To anyone who might care.

Verse 2

Dmaj7　　　**E**　　│　　　│ **C♯m**
　　Thought I could fly,
　　　　　Dmaj7│　　　│
So I stepped off the　Golden, mm.
　　　E　│　　│ **C♯m**
No - body cried,
　　　　Dmaj7│
Nobody even　　noticed.
　　　　　│　　　　　**E**│
I saw them standing right there,
　　　　　│ **C♯m**　　　**Dmaj7**│　　　　‖
Kinda thought they might care.

Pre-Chorus 1

Dmaj7 E | |C#m
　　　　I had a dream

　　　　　　Dmaj7 |
I got ev'ry - thing I   wanted.

　　|　　　　　**E | |**
But when I wake up, I see

C#m   Dmaj7 |
You with me.

Chorus 1

　　　　　　　‖Dmaj7   E | |C#m
And you say, "As long as I'm here, __

　　　　Dmaj7 | |
No one can   hurt you.

　　　　　　E | |C#m
Don't want to lie here, __

　　　　Dmaj7 | |
But you can   learn to.

　　E |
If I could change

　　　　|**C#7   Dmaj7 | |**
The way that you   see yourself,

　　　　　　　E | |C#m
You wouldn't won - der why you're here. __

　　　　Dmaj7 | ‖
They don't deserve you."

Verse 3

Dmaj7 |E |C#m
　　I tried to scream,

　　　　　　　|Dmaj7 |
But my head was under - water.

　　　　　　　|E |C#m
They called me weak,

　　　　　　　　　　|Dmaj7
Like I'm not just somebody's daughter.

　N.C. |Dmaj7   E |
It could have been a nightmare,

　　　　　　　　　|C#m   Dmaj7 |
But it felt like they were right there.

Bridge

```
 ‖Dmaj7                       |E
And it feels like yesterday was a year ago,
  |C♯m                |Dmaj7
But I don't want to let any - body know.
     |                         |E
'Cause ev'rybody wants something from me now,
    |C♯m                          |Dmaj7        ‖
And I don't want to let them down.
```

Pre-Chorus 2   *Repeat Pre-Chorus 1*

Chorus 2   *Repeat Chorus 1*

Outro

```
Dmaj7      E    |                      |C♯m
If I knew it all then, would I do it again,
                  |Dmaj7      |
Would I do it again?
               E      |                       |C♯m
If they knew what they said would go straight to my head,
                 |Dmaj7      |
What would they say instead?
               E    |              |C♯7
If I knew it all then, would I do it again,
                 |Dmaj7      |
Would I do it again?
               E      |                       |C♯7
If they knew what they said would go straight to my head,
                    |Dmaj7       |             |
What would they say instead?
E             |C♯m         |Dmaj7        ‖
```

Bellyache

Words and Music by
Billie Eilish O'Connell and Finneas O'Connell

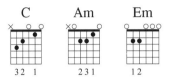

Intro

N.C.(C) |(Am) |
Mind, _____

Em | |
Mind.

C |Am |Em | ||

Verse 1

C |
Sittin' all alone,

Am
Mouth full of gum

  |Em |
In the driveway.

 |C
My friends aren't far,

  |Am
In the back of my car

  |Em |
Lay their bodies.

   |C |Am
Where's my mind? __

    |Em |
Where's my mind?

Verse 2

```
        ‖C                     |
They'll be here pretty soon,
Am
Lookin' through my room
        |Em       |
For the money.
      |C
I'm bitin' my nails.
        |Am
I'm too young to go to jail,
        |Em        |
It's kinda funny.
             |C      |Am
Where's my mind? __
             |Em    |
Where's my mind?
             |C      |Am
Where's my mind? __
             |Em    |
Where is my mind?
```

Chorus 1

```
N.C.           ‖C
Maybe it's in the gutter,
              |Am
Where I left my lover.
                   |Em         |
What an expensive __ fate.
                |C
My V is for Ven - detta.
                |Am
Thought that I'd feel better
      N.C.               |Em     |         ‖
And now I've got a bellyache.
```

9

Verse 3

C
Ev'rything I do,

    |Am
The way I wear my noose

       |Em |
Like a necklace.

 |C
I wanna make 'em scared,

      |Am
Like I could be anywhere,

        |Em |
Like I'm reckless.

        |C |Am
I lost my mind. __

      |Em |
I don't mind.

         |C |Am
Where's my mind? __

         |Em |
Where's my mind?

Chorus 2

N.C. ‖ **C**
Maybe it's in the gutter,

|**Am**
Where I left my lover.

|**Em** |
What an expensive __ fate.

|**C**
My V is for Ven - detta.

|**Am**
Thought that I'd feel better

N.C. |
And now I've got a bellyache.

Em |
 (Bellyache, bellyache, bellyache, bellyache,

Bellyache, bellyache.)

Chorus 3

N.C. ‖ **C**
Maybe it's in the gutter

|**Am**
Where I left my lover.

|**Em** |
What an expensive __ fate.

|**C**
My V is for Ven - detta.

|**Am**
Thought that I'd feel better

N.C. ‖
And now I've got a bellyache.

I Love You

Words and Music by
Billie Eilish O'Connell and Finneas O'Connell

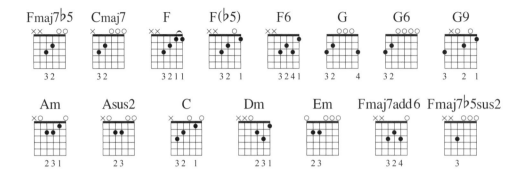

Intro   Fmaj7♭5 | |Cmaj7 |

Verse 1   ‖Fmaj7♭5 |
It's not true.
        |Cmaj7 |
Tell me I've been lied to.
    |Fmaj7♭5 |
Crying isn't like you.
  |Cmaj7 |
Oo. __
        |Fmaj7♭5 |
What the hell did I do?
      |Cmaj7 |
Never been the type to
        |Fmaj7♭5 |
Let someone see right through.
    |Cmaj7 |
Oo. __
                    ‖
Mm, hmm, mm, hmm.

Chorus 1

  F   F(♭5)
Maybe, won't you take it back,
     |F |F6
Say you were trying to make me laugh;
      |G |G6
And nothing has to change today:
     |G9   G |Am |Asus2
You didn't mean to say, "I love you."
    |C |Cmaj7
I love you,
                    |Fmaj7 |Fmaj7♭5
And I don't want to.
    |Cmaj7
Oo. __

Verse 2

    ‖Fmaj7♭5 |
Up all night
        |Cmaj7 |
On another redeye.
              |Fmaj7♭5 |
I wish we'd never learned to fly,
    |Cmaj7 |
I. __
              |Fmaj7♭5 |
Maybe we should just try
           |Cmaj7 |
To tell ourselves a good lie.
        |Fmaj7♭5 |
Didn't mean to make you cry,
   |Cmaj7 |
I. __
                    ‖
Mm, hmm, mm, hmm.

Chorus 2   *Repeat Chorus 1*

Bridge

‖ **Dm7**
The smile that you gave me,

    | **Em** | **Fmaj7** | **Fmaj7add6**
Even when you felt like dy - in'.

Chorus 3

‖ **F**   **F(♭5)**
We fall apart as it gets dark.

   | **F** | **F6**
I'm in your arms in Central Park.

    | **G**   **G6**
There's nothing you could do or say.

  | **G9**   **G** | **Am** | **Asus2**
I can't escape the way I love you.

       | **Cmaj7** |
I don't want to,

      | **Fmaj7♭5**   **Fmaj7** | **Fmaj7♭5**
But I love you.

   | **Cmaj7** |
Oo. __

          ‖
Oo. __

Outro

Fmaj7♭5 |

   | **Cmaj7** |
Oo. __

   | **Fmaj7♭5sus2** |
Oo. __

   | **N.C.**   ‖
Oo. __

Idontwannabeyouanymore

Words and Music by
Billie Eilish O'Connell and Finneas O'Connell

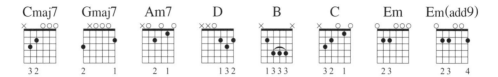

Intro

Cmaj7 | |Gmaj7 |

|**Am7** |

By, di, da, die, da.

|**Gmaj7** | ||

By, di, da, die, da.

Verse 1

Cmaj7 |

Don't be that way,

|**Gmaj7** |

Fall a - part twice a day.

|**Am7** | |**Gmaj7**

I just wish you could feel what you

| |

Say.

Cmaj7 |

Show, never tell;

|**Gmaj7** |

But I know you too well,

|**Am7** | |**D** |

Kind of mood that you wish you could sell.

Chorus 1

‖**Cmaj7** |

If teardrops could be bottled,

|**Gmaj7** |

There'd be swimming pools filled by models

|**Am7** | |**B** |

Told a tight dress is what makes you a whore.

|**Cmaj7** |

If "I love you" was a promise

|**Gmaj7** |

Would you break it if you're honest,

|**Am** | |**D** | |

Tell the mirror what you know she's heard be - fore?

C | |**B** |**N.C.** |

I don't wanna be you

|**Em** | | | ‖

Any - more.

Verse 2

Cmaj7 |

Hands getting cold,

|**Gmaj7** |

Losing feeling is getting old.

|**Am7** | |**Gmaj7** | |

Was I made from a broken mold?

Cmaj7 |

Hurt I can't shake,

|**Gmaj7** |

We've made ev'ry mistake.

|**Am7** | |**D** |

Only you know the way that I ____ break, uh.

Chorus 2

‖**Cmaj7** |
If teardrops could be bottled,

|**Gmaj7** |
There'd be swimming pools filled by models

|**Am7** | |**B** |
Told a tight dress is what makes you a whore.

|**Cmaj7** |
If "I love you" was a promise

|**Gmaj7** |
Would you break it if you're honest,

|**Am7** | |**D** | |
Tell the mirror what you know she's heard be - fore?

C | |**B** | |
I don't wanna be you.

C | |**B** | |
I don't wanna be you.

C | |**B** |
I don't wanna be you

|**Em(add9)** ‖
Any - more.

Lovely

Words and Music by Billie Eilish O'Connell,
Finneas O'Connell and Khalid Robinson

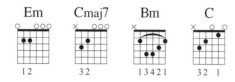

Intro

Em | |Cmaj7 | |

Em |Bm |C | |

Em |Bm ||

Verse 1

C | |
Thought I found a way,

Em |Bm
Thought I found a way out.

  |C |
But you never go away,

  |Em |Bm
So I guess I gotta stay now.

Pre-Chorus 1

      ||Cmaj7
Oh, I hope some - day

  | |Em |Bm
I'll make it out of here,

    |Cmaj7 |
Even if it takes all night

  |Em |Bm
Or a hundred years.

    |Cmaj7
Need a place to hide,

  | |Em |Bm
But I can't find one near.

    |Cmaj7
Wanna feel a - live,

  | |Em |Bm
Outside I can't fight my fear.

Chorus 1

Cmaj7 | |
Isn't it lovely, all alone?

Em |**Bm** |
Heart made of glass, my mind of stone.

Cmaj7 | |**Em**
Tear me to pieces, skin to bone.

|**Bm** |**C** | ||
Hello, welcome home.

Verse 2

C | |
Walking out of time,

Em |**Bm** |
Looking for a better place.

C | |
Something's on my mind,

Em |**Bm**
Always in my head space.

Pre-Chorus 2

||**Cmaj7**
But I know some - day

| |**Em** |**Bm**
I'll make it out of here,

|**Cmaj7** |
Even if it takes all night

|**Em** |**Bm**
Or a hundred years.

|**Cmaj7**
Need a place to hide,

| |**Em** |**Bm**
But I can't find one near.

|**Cmaj7**
Wanna feel a - live,

| |**Em** |**Bm** ||
Outside I can't fight my fear.

Chorus 2

Cmaj7 | |
Isn't it lovely, all alone?

Em |Bm |
Heart made of glass, my mind of stone.

Cmaj7 | |Em
Tear me to pieces, skin to bone.

  |Bm ‖
Hello, welcome home.

Verse 3

Cmaj7 |

  |Em |Bm |
Oh, __ yeah. __

C |
Yeah,

  |Em |
Ah. __

Bm ‖
Oh, oh.

Outro

Cmaj7 | |Em |

Bm |Cmaj7 | |Em

  |Bm |C ‖
Hello, welcome home. __

My Future

Words and Music by
Billie Eilish O'Connell and Finneas O'Connell

(Capo 1st fret)

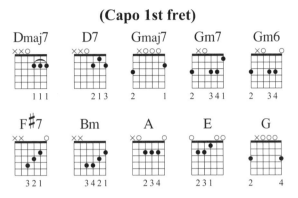

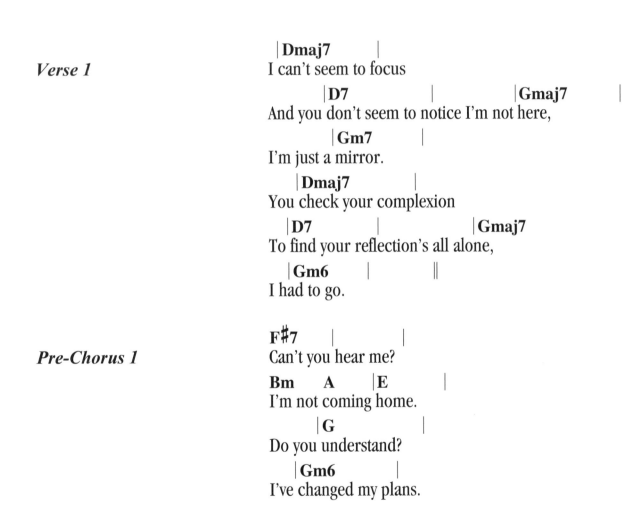

Verse 1

|**Dmaj7** |
I can't seem to focus

|**D7** | |**Gmaj7** |
And you don't seem to notice I'm not here,

|**Gm7** |
I'm just a mirror.

|**Dmaj7** |
You check your complexion

|**D7** | |**Gmaj7**
To find your reflection's all alone,

|**Gm6** | ‖
I had to go.

Pre-Chorus 1

F♯7 | |
Can't you hear me?

Bm **A** |**E** |
I'm not coming home.

|**G** |
Do you understand?

|**Gm6** |
I've changed my plans.

Chorus 1

‖**Dmaj7** |
'Cause I,

|**D7** |
I'm in love

|**Gmaj7** |
With my future,

|**Gm7** |
Can't wait to meet her.

|**Dmaj7** |
And I,

|**D7** |
I'm in love

|**Gmaj7** |
But not with an - ybody else,

|**Gm7** | ‖
Just wanna get to know myself.

Interlude

|**Dmaj7** | ‖

Verse 2

Dmaj7 | |**D7**
  I know, supposedly, I'm lonely now,

| |**Gmaj7** |
Know I'm supposed to be un - happy without someone.

|**Gm7** | |
But aren't I someone?

Dmaj7 | |**D7** | |
I'd   like

|**Gmaj7** |
To be your answer.

|**Gm7** |
'Cause you're so handsome.

22

Pre-Chorus 2

‖**F♯7** | |
But I know better

Bm **A** |**E** |
Than to drive you home.

|**G** |
'Cause you'd in - vite me in

|**Gm6** |
And I'd be yours again.

Chorus 2

‖**Dmaj7** |
But I,

|**D7** |
I'm in love

|**Gmaj7** |
With my future

|**Gm7** |
And you don't know her, oo,

|**Dmaj7** |
And I,

|**D7** |
I'm in love,

|**Gmaj7** |
But not with any - body else here.

|**Gm7** | |**Dmaj7** ‖
I'll see you in a couple years. _____

No Time to Die

from NO TIME TO DIE

Words and Music by
Billie Eilish O'Connell and Finneas O'Connell

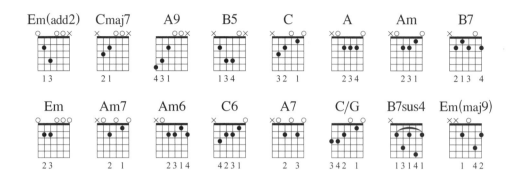

Intro

|Em(add2) |Cmaj7 |A9 |B5 |

|Em(add2) |Cmaj7 |A9 |B5 ||

Verse 1

Em(add2) C |A   Am |Em(add2)
      I should have known

  C |A   Am |Em(add2)
I'd leave alone.

  C |A   Am
Just goes to show

     |C
That the blood you bleed

           |B7
Is just the blood you own.

Verse 2

Em(add2) C |A   Am |Em(add2)
      We were a pair,

  C |A   Am |Em(add2)
But I saw you there.

  C |A   Am
Too much to bear.

     |C
You were my life,

         |B7
But life is far away from fair.

Pre-Chorus 1

‖**C**
Was I stupid to love you?

|**Em**
Was I reckless to help?

|**Am7** |**B7**
Was it obvious to everybody else

Chorus 1

‖**Em(add2)** **C** |**Am**
That I'd fallen   for a lie?

|**Em(add2)** **C** |**Am**
You were never   on my side.

|**Em**   **C**
Fool me once, fool me twice.

|**Am**
Are you death or paradise?

|**Em** **C** |**Am6**
Now you'll never see me cry,

‖
There's just no time to die.

Interlude

|**Em(add2)** |**Cmaj7** |**A9** |**B7**   ‖

Verse 3

Em(add2) **C** |**A**   **Am** |**Em(add2)**
        I let it burn

            C |**A**   **Am** |**Em(add2)**
That you're no longer my con - cern.

     C |**A**   **Am**
Faces from my past return,

|**C** |**B7**
Another lesson yet to learn,

Chorus 2

‖**Em(add2) C** |**Am**
That I'd fallen   for a lie.

|**Em(add2) C** |**Am**
You were never   on my side.

|**Em**   **C**
Fool me once, fool me twice.

|**Am**
Are you death or paradise?

|**Em   C** |**Am**
Now you'll never see me cry,

|**Em** |**C6**
There's just no time to die.

|**A7**
No time to die.

|**B7** |**Em** |**C/G**
Mm, no time to die.

|**A** |**B7sus4**
Mm.

|**Em**   **C**
Fool me once, fool me twice.

|**Am**
Are you death or paradise?

|**Em   C** |**Am**
Now you'll never see me cry,

|**Em**   **Em(maj9)**   ‖
There's just no time to die.

When The Party's Over

Words and Music by
Finneas O'Connell

(Capo 2nd fret)

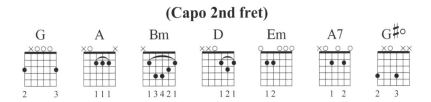

G   A   Bm   D   Em   A7   G#°

Intro 1

‖: **G**   **A** |**Bm**   **A** |**D**   **A** |
Mm. _____

G |**N.C.** | :‖
_____

Verse 1

G **A** |**Bm** **A** |
Don't you know I'm

D **A** |**G** | |
No good for you?

     | **A** |**Bm** **A** |
I've learned to   lose you,

D **A** |**G** | | |
Can't af - ford to.

      A |**Bm** **A** |
Tore my shirt to

D **A** |**G** | |
Stop you bleeding.

   | **A** |**Bm** **A** |
But noth - in' ev - er

D **A** |**G** | | |
Stops you leavin'.

          |**Bm**
Quiet when I'm comin' home,

A |**D** **A** |**G** | ‖
I'm on my own.

Chorus 1

Em |Bm |
I could lie, say I like it like that,
D |G | |
Like it like that.
Em |Bm |
I could lie, say I like it like that.
D |G | | | ‖
Like it like that.

Verse 2

G   A |Bm A |
Don't you know too
D   A |G | |
Much al - ready?
   | A |Bm A |
I'll on - ly hurt you.
D A |G | | |
If you let me.
    A |Bm
Call me friend,
A |D   A |G |
But keep me closer.
N.C.(D) |
(Call me back.)
     |G A |Bm A |
And I'll call you when the
D   A |G N.C.| | |
Par - ty's over.
G   A |Bm
Quiet when I'm comin' home,
A |D A |G |
I'm on my own.

Chorus 2

‖**Em** |**Bm** |

And I could lie, say I like it like that,

D |**G** |

Like it like that.

     |**Em** |**Bm** |

Yeah, I could lie, say I like it like that.

D |**G** |

Like it like that.

     |**Em** |**Bm** |**D** |**G** |

But nothin' is better some - times.

Em |**Bm** |**D** |**G** | |

Once we've both said our good - byes, _____

A7 | |**G** |**G♯°**

Let's just let it go.

     |**A7** | |**G** | | | ‖

And let me let you   go.

Outro

G |**Bm**

Quiet when I'm comin' home,

     |**D** |**G** | |

I'm on my   own.

Em |**Bm** |

I could lie, say I like it like that,

D |**G** | |

Like it like that.

Em |**Bm** |

I could lie, say I like it like that,

D |**N.C.** **G** ‖

Like it like that.

Ocean Eyes

Words and Music by
Finneas O'Connell

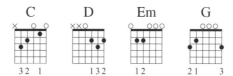

Intro

C   D   Em |
Ahh, _____

C   D   Em |
Ahh, _____

C   D   Em |
Ahh, _____

G   C   ‖
Ahh. ___

Verse 1

C   D   Em |C   D   Em |
I've been watching you for some time.

C   D   Em |G   C |
Can't stop starin' at those ocean eyes.

     D   Em |C   D   Em |
Burn - ing cities and na - palm skies.

C   D   Em |G   C
Fif - teen flares inside those ocean eyes,

    |G   C
Your ocean eyes.

Chorus 1

```
        ‖C  D  Em  |C  D  Em
No fair. _____
              |C          D        Em
You really know how to make me cry
                          |G      C
When you give me those ocean eyes.
          |C  D  Em |C  D  Em
I'm scared. _____
              |C          D        Em
I've never fallen from quite this high.
                  |G      C
Falling into your ocean eyes,
        |G      C      ‖
Those ocean eyes.
```

Verse 2

```
        C   D   Em              |C      D      Em   |
I've been walking through a world gone blind.
        C   D   Em          |G          C    |
Can't stop thinkin' of your diamond mine.
              D   Em          |C      D      Em
Care - ful creature made friends with time.
        |C  D  Em          |G          C
He left her lonely with a diamond mine
              |G      C
And those ocean eyes.
```

Chorus 2

Repeat Chorus 1

Interlude

```
‖: C  D  Em  |C  D  Em  |C  D  Em  |C  D  Em  |G      C  :‖G      C
```

Chorus 3

Repeat Chorus 1

Six Feet Under

Words and Music by
Finneas O'Connell

Bm	A	G	Gmaj7	Em	E

Verse 1

Bm |**A** |**G** |**A**
Help; I lost myself a - gain,

    |**Bm** |**A** |**G** | |
But I ___ remember you.

Bm |**A** |**G** |**A**
Don't come back; it won't end well,

    |**Bm** |**A** |**G** |
But I wish you'd tell me to.

Chorus 1

    ‖**Bm** |**A**
Our love is six feet under.

    |**Gmaj7** |**A**
I can't help but wonder

    |**Bm** |**A** |**Em** |
If our grave was watered by the rain,

    |**G** | **A** |**Bm** |
Would roses bloom? _____

    |**G** | **A** |**Bm** |**A**
Could roses bloom _____

    |**Gmaj7** |
Again?

Verse 2

    ‖**Bm** |**A**
Retrace my lips

    |**G** |**A** |
Erase your touch.

    |**Bm** |**A** |**G** |
It's all too much for me.

Bm |**A** |**G** |**A**
Blow a - way like smoke in air.

    |**Bm** |**A** |**G** |**N.C.**
How can you die careless - ly?

Chorus 2

‖ **Bm** |**A**
Our love is six feet under.

|**Gmaj7** |**A**
I can't help but wonder

|**Bm** |**A** |**Em** |
If our grave was watered by the rain,

|**G** | **A** |**Bm** |
Would roses bloom? _____

|**G** | **A** |**Bm** |**A**
Could roses bloom? _____

Bridge

‖ **G** |
They're playing our sound,

A |**Bm** |
Laying us down tonight.

|**G** |**A** |**Bm** |**A**
And all of these clouds crying us back to life,

|**G** | ‖
But you're cold as the night.

Chorus 3

Bm |**A**
Six feet under.

|**G** |**A**
I can't help but wonder

|**Bm** |**A** |**Em** | |
If our grave was watered by the rain…

G | **A** |**Bm** | |
Bloom. _____

G | **A** |**Bm** |**A**
Bloom _____

|**Gmaj7** | | | ‖
Again.

Outro

Bm |**A** |**G** |**A**
Help; I lost myself a - gain,

|**Bm** |**A** |**G** ‖
But I ____ remember you.

Therefore I Am

Words and Music by
Billie Eilish O'Connell and Finneas O'Connell

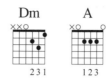

Chorus 1

N.C. ‖Dm |
I'm not your friend, or anything.

|A
Damn, you think that you're the man.

|
I think, therefore I am.

|Dm |
I'm not your friend, or anything.

|A
Damn, you think that you're the man.

| ‖
I think, therefore I am.

Verse 1

N.C. |(Dm)
Stop. What the hell are you talking a - bout?

|(A)
Ha! Get my pretty name outta your mouth.

|
We are not the same, with or without.

|Dm |
Don't talk 'bout me like how you might know how I feel.

|A
Top of the world, but your world isn't real.

|
Your world's an ideal.

|N.C.
So, go have fun.

|
I really couldn't care less, and you can give 'em my best,

But just know...

Chorus 2

Repeat Chorus 1

Verse 2

N.C.(Dm) |

    I don't want press to put your name next to mine.

                                  |(A)

We're on diff'rent lines, so I

                      |

Wanna be nice enough they don't call my bluff.

                  |Dm

'Cause I hate to find

                  |

Articles, articles, articles.

                                    |(A)

Rather you remain unremarkable. (Got a lotta)

                        |

Interviews, interviews, interviews.

When they say your name, I just act confused.

           |

Did you have fun?

I really couldn't care less,

           |

And you can give 'em my best, but just know…

Chorus 3

N.C.   ‖Dm |

    I'm not your friend, or anything.

                        |A

Damn, you think that you're the man.

                  |

I think, therefore I am.

             |Dm |

I'm not your friend, or anything.

                        |A

Damn, you think that you're the man.

                  |

I think, therefore I am.

Bridge

       ‖Dm |

I'm sorry,

                    |A |

I don't think I caught your name.

       |Dm |

I'm sorry,

                    |A | |

I don't think I caught your name. _____

Dm | |A | |

Outro-Chorus

Repeat Chorus 1

Wish You Were Gay

Words and Music by
Billie Eilish O'Connell and Finneas O'Connell

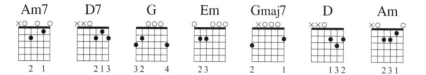

Verse 1

‖**Am7**   **D7**
"Baby, I don't feel so good,"

|**G**   **Em**
Six words you never understood.

|**Am7**
"I'll never let you go,"

D7 |**G**   **Em**
Five words you'll never say.

|**Am7**   **D7**
I laugh a - lone like nothing's wrong,

|**Gmaj7**   **Em**
Four days has never felt so long.

|**Am7**   **D7**
If three's a crowd and two was us,

|**G**   ‖
One slipped away.

Chorus 1

Am7   D7 |Gmaj7   Em
I just wanna make you feel o - kay,
     |Am7   D7 |Gmaj7   Em |
But all you do is look the other way, mm.
Am7   D7 |Gmaj7   Em |
I can't tell you how much I wish I didn't wanna stay, mm.
Am7   D7 |G   N.C.
I just kinda wish you were gay.

Verse 2

         ‖Am7   D7
Is there a reason we're not through?
     |G   Em
Is there a twelve-step just for you?
      |Am7   D7
Our conver - sation's all in blue,
     |Gmaj7   Em
Eleven "heys."
     |Am7   D7
Ten fingers tearing out my hair,
      |Gmaj7   Em
Nine times you never made it there.
    |Am7   D7 |G   ‖
I ate a - lone at seven, you were six minutes away.

Chorus 2

N.C. |Gmaj7   Em
How am I s'posed to make you feel o - kay
     |Am7   D7 |Gmaj7 Em |
When all you do is walk the other way? Uh.
Am7   D7 |Gmaj7   Em |
I can't tell you how much I wish I didn't wanna stay, uh.
Am7   D7 |G
I just kinda wish you were gay.

Bridge

```
           ‖Am7    D7
To spare my pride,
                        |Gmaj7              Em
To give your lack of in  -  t'rest an explana - tion,
                   |Am7    D7
Don't say I'm not your type.
                          |Gmaj7              Em
Just say I'm not your pre - ferred sexual orienta - tion.
           |N.C.   D7
I'm so selfish,
                       |Gmaj7              Em
But you make me feel helpless, yeah.
              |Am7                    |
And I can't stand another day,
D7                         ‖
Stand another day.
```

Outro-Chorus

```
     Am7        D7              |Gmaj7
I just wanna make you feel o - kay,
      |Am7        D7              |G       |
But all you do is     look the other way, mm.
Am7           D7                     |Gmaj7    Em   |
I can't tell you how much I wish I didn't wanna stay, oh.
Am7        D7            |G     Em   |
I just kinda wish you were gay.
Am7        D7            |G     Em   |
I just kinda wish you were gay.
Am7        D7            |G           ‖
I just kinda wish you were gay.
```

STRUM & SING

Lyrics, chord symbols, and guitar chord diagrams for your favorite songs.

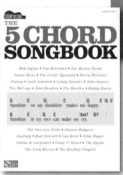

GUITAR

ACOUSTIC CLASSICS
00191891 .... $14.99

ADELE
00159855 .... $12.99

SARA BAREILLES
00102354 .... $12.99

THE BEATLES
00172234 .... $16.99

BLUES
00159335 .... $12.99

ZAC BROWN BAND
02501620 .... $14.99

COLBIE CAILLAT
02501725 .... $14.99

CAMPFIRE FOLK SONGS
02500686 .... $14.99

CHART HITS OF 2014-2015
00142554 .... $12.99

CHART HITS OF 2015-2016
00156248 .... $12.99

BEST OF KENNY CHESNEY
00142457 .... $14.99

CHRISTMAS SONGS
00171332 .... $14.99

KELLY CLARKSON
00146384 .... $14.99

COFFEEHOUSE SONGS FOR GUITAR
00285991 .... $14.99

LEONARD COHEN
00265489 .... $14.99

JOHN DENVER COLLECTION
02500632 .... $12.99

DISNEY
00233900 .... $16.99

EAGLES
00157994 .... $12.99

EASY ACOUSTIC SONGS
00125478 .... $14.99

THE 5 CHORD SONGBOOK
02501718 .... $12.99

FOLK SONGS
02501482 .... $10.99

FOLK/ROCK FAVORITES
02501669 .... $12.99

FOUR CHORD SONGS
00249581 .... $14.99

THE 4 CHORD SONGBOOK
02501533 .... $12.99

THE 4-CHORD COUNTRY SONGBOOK
00114936 .... $15.99

THE GREATEST SHOWMAN
00278383 .... $14.99

HAMILTON
00217116 .... $14.99

JACK JOHNSON
02500858 .... $17.99

ROBERT JOHNSON
00191890 .... $12.99

CAROLE KING
00115243 .... $10.99

BEST OF GORDON LIGHTFOOT
00139393 .... $14.99

DAVE MATTHEWS BAND
02501078 .... $10.95

JOHN MAYER
02501636 .... $10.99

INGRID MICHAELSON
02501634 .... $10.99

THE MOST REQUESTED SONGS
02501748 .... $12.99

JASON MRAZ
02501452 .... $14.99

PRAISE & WORSHIP
00152381 .... $12.99

ELVIS PRESLEY
00198890 .... $12.99

QUEEN
00218578 .... $12.99

ROCK AROUND THE CLOCK
00103625 .... $12.99

ROCK BALLADS
02500872 .... $9.95

ROCKETMAN
00300469 .... $17.99

ED SHEERAN
00152016 .... $14.99

THE 6 CHORD SONGBOOK
02502277 .... $12.99

CAT STEVENS
00116827 .... $14.99

TAYLOR SWIFT
00159856 .... $12.99

THE 3 CHORD SONGBOOK
00211634 .... $10.99

TODAY'S HITS
00119301 .... $12.99

TOP CHRISTIAN HITS
00156331 .... $12.99

TOP HITS OF 2016
00194288 .... $12.99

KEITH URBAN
00118558 .... $14.99

THE WHO
00103667 .... $12.99

YESTERDAY
00301629 .... $14.99

NEIL YOUNG – GREATEST HITS
00138270 .... $14.99

UKULELE

THE BEATLES
00233899 .... $16.99

COLBIE CAILLAT
02501731 .... $10.99

COFFEEHOUSE SONGS FOR UKULELE
00138238 .... $14.99

JOHN DENVER
02501694 .... $10.99

FOLK ROCK FAVORITES FOR UKULELE
00114600 .... $12.99

THE 4-CHORD UKULELE SONGBOOK
00114331 .... $14.99

JACK JOHNSON
02501702 .... $19.99

JOHN MAYER
02501706 .... $10.99

INGRID MICHAELSON
02501741 .... $12.99

THE MOST REQUESTED SONGS
02501453 .... $14.99

JASON MRAZ
02501753 .... $14.99

SING-ALONG SONGS
02501710 .... $15.99

HAL•LEONARD®
www.halleonard.com
Visit our website to see full song lists.

Prices, content, and availability subject to change without notice.

Guitar Chord Songbooks

Each 6" x 9" book includes complete lyrics, chord symbols, and guitar chord diagrams.

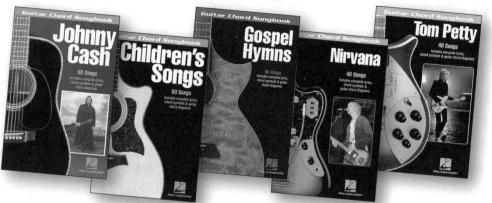

Acoustic Hits
00701787 . . . . $14.99

Acoustic Rock
00699540 . . . . $21.99

Alabama
00699914 . . . . $14.95

The Beach Boys
00699566 . . . . $19.99

The Beatles
00699562 . . . . $17.99

Bluegrass
00702585 . . . . $14.99

Johnny Cash
00699648 . . . . $17.99

Children's Songs
00699539 . . . . $16.99

Christmas Carols
00699536 . . . . $12.99

Christmas Songs
00119911 . . . . $14.99

Eric Clapton
00699567 . . . . $19.99

Classic Rock
00699598 . . . . $18.99

Coffeehouse Hits
00703318 . . . . $14.99

Country
00699534 . . . . $17.99

Country Favorites
00700609 . . . . $14.99

Country Hits
00140859 . . . . $14.99

Country Standards
00700608 . . . . $12.95

Cowboy Songs
00699636 . . . . $19.99

Creedence Clearwater Revival
00701786 . . . . $16.99

Jim Croce
00148087 . . . . $14.99

Crosby, Stills & Nash
00701609 . . . . $16.99

John Denver
02501697 . . . . $17.99

Neil Diamond
00700606 . . . . $19.99

Disney – 2nd Edition
00295786 . . . . $17.99

The Doors
00699888 . . . . $17.99

Eagles
00122917 . . . . $17.99

Early Rock
00699916 . . . . $14.99

Folksongs
00699541 . . . . $14.99

Folk Pop Rock
00699651 . . . . $17.99

40 Easy Strumming Songs
00115972 . . . . $16.99

Four Chord Songs
00701611 . . . . $14.99

Glee
00702501 . . . . $14.99

Gospel Hymns
00700463 . . . . $14.99

Grand Ole Opry®
00699885 . . . . $16.95

Grateful Dead
00139461 . . . . $14.99

Green Day
00103074 . . . . $14.99

Irish Songs
00701044 . . . . $14.99

Michael Jackson
00137847 . . . . $14.99

Billy Joel
00699632 . . . . $19.99

Elton John
00699732 . . . . $15.99

Ray LaMontagne
00130337 . . . . $12.99

Latin Songs
00700973 . . . . $14.99

Love Songs
00701043 . . . . $14.99

Bob Marley
00701704 . . . . $17.99

Bruno Mars
00125332 . . . . $12.99

Paul McCartney
00385035 . . . . $16.95

Steve Miller
00701146 . . . . $12.99

Modern Worship
00701801 . . . . $16.99

Motown
00699734 . . . . $17.99

Willie Nelson
00148273 . . . . $17.99

Nirvana
00699762 . . . . $16.99

Roy Orbison
00699752 . . . . $17.99

Peter, Paul & Mary
00103013 . . . . $19.99

Tom Petty
00699883 . . . . $15.99

Pink Floyd
00139116 . . . . $14.99

Pop/Rock
00699538 . . . . $16.99

Praise & Worship
00699634 . . . . $14.99

Elvis Presley
00699633 . . . . $17.99

Queen
00702395 . . . . $14.99

Red Hot Chili Peppers
00699710 . . . . $19.99

The Rolling Stones
00137716 . . . . $17.99

Bob Seger
00701147 . . . . $12.99

Carly Simon
00121011 . . . . $14.99

Sting
00699921 . . . . $17.99

Taylor Swift
00263755 . . . . $16.99

Three Chord Acoustic Songs
00123860 . . . . $14.99

Three Chord Songs
00699720 . . . . $17.99

Two-Chord Songs
00119236 . . . . $16.99

U2
00137744 . . . . $14.99

Hank Williams
00700607 . . . . $16.99

Stevie Wonder
00120862 . . . . $14.99

Prices and availability subject to change without notice.

Visit Hal Leonard online at **www.halleonard.com**

1120
9/12; 480